Monterey Bay
❖ Yesterday ❖

PUBLICATIONS
Betty Lewis

1974 – **VICTORIAN HOMES
OF WATSONSVILLE**
Pajaro Valley Historical Association

1975 – **WALKING & DRIVING
TOUR OF HISTORIC
WATSONVILLE**
(PAMPHLET) Sponsored by
Chamber of Commerce, CBID and
Pajaro Valley Historical Association
8th printing

1975 – **HIGHLIGHTS IN THE
HISTORY OF WATSONVILLE**
Watsonville Federal Savings &
Loan for their 50th Anniversary

1976 – **WATSONVILLE-MEMORIES
THAT LINGER**
Otter B Books, Santa Cruz

1977 – **MONTEREY BAY
YESTERDAY**
OTTER B BOOKS

1978 – **WATSONVILLE YESTERDAY**
Mehl's Colonial Chapel —
100 radio programs

1980 – **WATSONVILLE-MEMORIES
THAT LINGER Vol. II**
Western Tanager Press, Santa Cruz

1985 – **W.H. WEEKS, ARCHITECT**
Panorama West, Fresno

Monterey Bay Yesterday

A Nostalgic Era in Postcards

Featuring the works of Architect William H. Weeks

Betty Lewis

OTTER B BOOKS 1987

MONTEREY BAY YESTERDAY

Copyright © 1977
by
Betty Lewis

ISBN 0-9617681-1-8

Second Printing, 1987

Published by
OTTER B BOOKS
SANTA CRUZ, CALIFORNIA
Manufactured in the United States of America

DEDICATION

This book is dedicated

to

Sam Stark

Post card collector

par excellence

Sam Stark, former actor and longtime feature writer for *Variety*, is now retired and lives in Pebble Beach. Mr. Stark is the Honorary Curator of the Theatre Collection of the University Libraries at Stanford University. He is an advanced collector of post cards, having 750,000 in his private collection, and is considered one of the foremost authorities in the United States in this hobby of Deltiology.

CONTENTS

Carmel	1
Pacific Grove	8
Monterey	17
Salinas	33
Hollister	46
San Juan Bautista	47
Spreckels	49
Paraiso Springs	50
King City	51
Gilroy	52
Castroville	55
Tassajara	56
Watsonville	57
Capitola	75
Soquel	80
Santa Cruz	82
Santa Cruz Mountains	109
Miscellaneous	118
List of Sources	124

Preface

Old post cards are pure nostalgia for present day collectors, but for the sellers and dealers these cards have become a lucrative business. This commercial aspect is overcome for true and serious collectors by the many attractive view and greeting cards available through exchanging with each other or by low values—actually pennies for cards that most dealers will not handle.

The collecting of post cards reached its zenith between 1900 and 1914, when it was disrupted by the first World War. Now, once again, the post card craze is taking hold.

Most people are unaware that the *postal* card did not make its appearance until 1870, and that it was 1893 before the Souvenir Card and Private Mailing Card, later to be known as post cards, were permitted under the rulings of the Postal Union. A *postal* card is purchased pre-stamped at a post office while a *post* card has the correct stamp affixed at the time of mailing. Until 1907, when the divided-back card was allowed, it was necessary to write the message on the view side, with only the name and address of the recipient on the opposite side. These restrictions were world-wide and enforced by the International Postal Union and the various governments that were members.

Post card collecting enjoyed a vogue that became a craze in the early 1900s with not only view cards and greetings but with the appearance of novelty cards. The latter were cards made of leather, cork, peat, metal or birch bark; some were decorated with plush, beads, metal objects or embellished with fur, feathers, real hair or tinselling. Leather cards were especially popular; when a sufficient number had been accumulated, holes could be punched along the borders and the cards laced together with thongs to form a pillow cover, an apron, or a wall hanging. Soon the delightful hold-to-light cards appeared. These cards, with often brilliant colorings, were to be held to a light which would reveal decorated Christmas trees, stained glass windows, ocean liners or tall buildings all aglow. Still other concealed hidden sentimental messages meant only for a sweetheart to read.

World War I saw a decline in post card collecting, mainly

because the dyes were in short supply and also because many of the finer cards were lithographed in Germany.

The hobby has been revived in recent years, with many local, state and national clubs in the United States, Canada, Great Britain and Europe. The latest listing of the Postcard Club Federation shows twenty-five clubs in the United States and England. The members hold monthly meetings, publish bulletins with detailed information and check lists of post cards, and supply rosters of members which enable those interested to exchange or buy and sell cards. In addition there are quite a few national auctions held each year which aid collectors in filling in sets or obtaining rare and elusive cards. Many of the long-time post card collectors bemoan this commercial aspect of their hobby, but the serious and resourceful collector can find antique shops, flea markets and garage sales where cards can be purchased cheaply.

Sam Stark

PICTURESQUE BUSINESS DISTRICT, CARMEL, CALIFORNIA—M19

CARMEL

Carmel-by-the-Sea is located four miles from Monterey and had its beginning as an artist colony. In 1903, J. Frank Devendorf and Frank Powers formed the Carmel Development Company. A charming town of quaint cottages and fascinating shops, it's a must for visitors to the area.

"Carmel Highlands, five miles south of Carmel on the new Coast Highway, which when completed will connect the Monterey Peninsula with Santa Barbara and Los Angeles via San Simeon. Here mountain, forest and sea blend in an unforgettable combination of scenic grandeur."—from a post card dated 1939

A Carmel Highlands Studio   Carmel, California

Forest Theatre, Carmel, California.   6221

Pacific Novelty Co., Pub.

Founded in 1910 by Herbert Heron, the Forest Theater in Carmel has been a popular outdoor theatre over the years—both with local residents and visitors to the area. They have seen such plays as *The Toad, Aladdin, Much Ado About Nothing*, and *Twelfth Night*, to name a few.

L. S. Slevin, Pub.

"The Forest Theatre at Carmel has won a notable place in the few years since its foundation. In part the outgrowth of the literary and art colony, it is the scene of dramatic productions every summer. The theatre is in the open, on a wooded hillside, whose slope forms the auditorium and whose trees—the distinctive trees of the peninsula—are the scenery."—"Monterey County, California," *Sunset*, 1912

CARMEL HIGHLANDS INN
Carmel Calif

SLEVIN PHOTO

Main Parlor Pine Inn Carmel-by-the-Sea

3

"Carmel - A village of more than 3,000 permanent inhabitants and known the world over. A Paradox village—built close to a pine and oak forested slope that faces westward to the sea. A community of the artist, the writer, the poet, the scientist, the painter, the playwright, a creative community outstandingly different from other small towns—unique, unusual and picturesque."—from a post card dated 1947

PINE INN, CARMEL, CAL.

L. S. Slevin, Pub.

Albertype Co., Pub.

HOTEL LA PLAYA, THE STRAND, CARMEL-BY-THE-SEA, CALIFORNIA.

FIRE PROOF, LARGE ROOMS, PRIVATE BATHS, VIEW OF OCEAN.

PUBL. BY CARMEL-BY-THE-SEA PHARMACY.

The Lodge Pebble Beach, 17 Mile Drive, Monterey Co, Calif.

4715

"Pebble Beach, facing Carmel Bay, is on Seventeen-Mile Drive, five miles from Monterey and Pacific Grove. Pebble Beach Lodge, built by the Pacific Improvement Company for assembly purposes, is operated as an adjunct of Del Monte. A park along the edge of the beach gives all residents free access to the shore. Pebble Beach has been divided into home sites of from one and a half to twenty acres."—"Monterey County, California." *Sunset*, 1912

Granite fireplace in Great Hall of Pebble Beach Lodge.

"The 17 Mile Drive is without question one of the most notable drives in the world. The drive passes through old Monterey, Pacific Grove and along the rugged coast line of Monterey Peninsula, with its famous cypress forests, moss beach, Pt. Joe, bird rock, fanshell beach and the lone cypress on midway point. Pebble Beach and Del Monte Lodge and many other points of interest worthy of a separate visit."—B. W. White, Monterey

1550 – ROAD THROUGH CYPRESS GROVE, SEVENTEEN MILE DRIVE, NEAR MONTEREY, CALIFORNIA. ON LINE OF

Edw. H. Mitchell, Pub.

B. W. White, Pub.

64   MISSION DEL RIO CARMELO, NEAR CARMEL, CALIFORNIA

115820

Founded in 1770, this mission was named for San Carlos (Saint Charles), son of an Italian nobleman who became a priest. He died in 1584 and was canonized in 1610. The Mission, which had been moved close to the Carmel River in 1771, was completely in ruins by 1884 when work was started on its restoration.

6

GOLF LINKS — PEBBLE BEACH   DEL MONTE, CALIFORNIA

The Albertype Co., Pub.

3052 — Mission San Carlos Borromeo (Carmel) Monterey County, California.

BURIAL PLACE OF PADRE JUNIPERO SERRA   FOUNDED 1770

Edw. H. Mitchell, Pub.

PACIFIC GROVE

"In 1873 a Methodist minister by the name of Ross, and his wife, both being in feeble health, having tried all the remedies that science could suggest, were advised to find some place where the temperature varied by little through the entire year, and where the fluctuations from heat to cold were merely nominal. After many months spent in research, it was at last decided that Pacific Grove was the most likely place to supply those requirements."—A. C. Jochmus, Pacific Grove *Review*

3049 – General View of Pacific Grove, California.

Edw. H. Mitchell, Pub.

Edw. H. Mitchell, Pub.

3040   25 8Mile Auto Boulevard, Pacific Grove, California

"The Seventeen Mile Drive begins and ends at Del Monte Hotel and encircles the whole Peninsula. It runs through Monterey, Pacific Grove, Pebble Beach, and back to the hotel. It passes through a seven-thousand-acre park, a park now divided into Villa sites, reached by a system of driveways all enjoyed by the public under reasonable restrictions."—Watkins, *History of Monterey. & Santa Cruz Counties, California*, 1925

3043 — Japanese Tea Garden, from Breakwater, Pacific Grove, California.

Edw. H. Mitchell, Pub.

Lover's Point area which also sported a large bathhouse, Japanese Tea Garden and bathing beach. There were also band concerts held on the beach with visitors and residents alike enjoying the music. The sign on the beach reads: "No person will be allowed to appear in tights or Jerseys only."

3042 — Lovers Point and the Breakwater, Pacific Grove, California.

Edw. H. Mitchell, Pub.

"Pacific Grove is a delightful resort community that offers much in recreation to entertain the visitor. It is famous as the Home of the Butterflies and for its floral and marine gardens, beaches, weird coastal rock formations and renowned municipal museum."—Bell Magazine Agency, Pacific Grove

Cardinell-Vincent Co., Pub.

NEW CONCRETE PIER AT BEACH, PACIFIC GROVE, CAL.
GLASS-BOTTOM BOAT AND EXCURSION LAUNCH.

Edw. H. Mitchell, Pub.

"Come to Pacific Grove - Where nature has planned new pleasures for every day. Splendid fishing, boating, bathing, submarine gardens, glass bottom boats, 100 miles of incomparable scenic automobile drives, primeval forest, sea shore beaches. Ideal Summer and Winter resort. Write Chamber of Commerce."—on back of post card

RAND CONCERT ON BEACH. PACIFIC GROVE, CAL.   S-455

HIGH SCHOOL - PACIFIC GROVE, CAL.   S-458

The Pacific Grove High School, designed by William H. Weeks, was built in 1906.

This seventeen-room mansion was built in 1896—a reproduction of the old Tennant house in Virginia. Used for educational and philanthropic purposes for sixty-seven years, the building was demolished in 1964 and the Canterbury Woods Retirement Residence was constructed, opening its doors in April of 1965.

Post card is dated 1912 and reads: "Don't let them work you too hard. One grand time in Pacific Grove."

1770 Tennant Memorial Home, Pacific Grove, California

3047 – Methodist Episcopal Church,
Pacific Grove, California.

This Gothic structure was built in 1888 on Lighthouse Avenue between 17th and 18th Streets. The church had a lighted cross that revolved and beamed its light far out to sea. A new church was built in 1962.

3046 – Carnegie Public Library, Pacific Grove, California.

The Pacific Grove Library was built in 1907 with a grant of $10,000 from Andrew Carnegie, and the architects were the McDougall Brothers. The library, with additions, is still in use.

Street Scene, Pacific Grove, Cal.

M. Reider, Pub.

The main street of Pacific Grove in 1908. The message on back of the post card reads: "No saloons in this town. Arrived here at 8 P.M. We are stopping at the Winton. It is next to the big Methodist Church and Assembly Hall. You can see the spires on the right hand side of the street, the two on horseback are in front of the hotel."

On the right is the same scene as above from a different angle showing more of the streetcar track which ran to Monterey.

3045 — Light House Avenue. Pacific Grove. California.

Edw. H. Mitchell, Pub.

Dated 1910, this post card reads: "Dear Emily: We won't leave any crabs for you, but instead you can have the fleas. Tomorrow I will go to Del Monte to take another lesson in swimming. I like to swim in this water, it is much nicer than at home."—sent to Sacramento

3048 - Pacific Grove Hotel, Pacific Grove, California.

Bird's-eye View, PACIFIC-GROVE, Cal.

The Pacific Grove Hotel, in the background of the post card on the left, was run in conjunction with the famed Del Monte Hotel of Monterey.

Lighthouse Avenue, Pacific Grove, California. 6680

Pacific Novelty Co., Pub.

A later view of Lighthouse Avenue showing the movie theatre in the background and the Winton Hotel adjacent with a flag on top.

Built in 1925, the Forest Hill Hotel was owned and operated by developer Samuel Parsons. In 1955, it became the property of the California-Nevada Methodist Church, Inc., and was converted as the Forest Hill Manor retirement home.

Forest Hill Hotel, Pacific Grove, California. 607?

Pacific Novelty Co., Pub.

1617:—Holman's Dep't Store, Pacific Grove, Calif.

"Holman's - Established 1891 - 46 departments, 100,000 sq. ft. of floor space, 360 feet of show window, four floors and daylight basement. We sell everything that men, women and children use, wear or eat. Branch buying offices in New York and San Francisco."—on back of post card

M. Kashower Co., Pub.

Publisher unknown

Souvenir from PACIFIC GROVE

268 – Monterey, California, in 1842
"BEFORE THE GRINGO CAME"

Edw. H. Mitchell, Pub.

MONTEREY

Newman Post Card Co., Pub.

Bird's-eye View of MONTEREY, Cal.

ROMAN PLUNGE AND SOLARIUM AT DEL MONTE, CALIFORNIA

Commercialchrome, Pub.

Detroit Publishing Co.

704 — ENTRANCE HOTEL DEL MONTE, MONTEREY COUNTY, CAL., COAST LINE, S. P. R. R.

8912. HOTEL DE

Edw. H. Mitchell, Pub.

Now the Naval School of Languages, the Hotel Del Monte was *the* place to stay in those glorious early years. With over 500 rooms, the hotel was situated on 250 acres of beautifully landscaped grounds which included 1,366 varieties of plant life. Guests could enjoy a round of golf, swimming in the tiled pool, a leisurely game of croquet, bowling on the green, or watching a rousing game of polo. The hotel was a favorite for honeymooners and vacationers, as well as for movie stars—such as W. C. Fields, Clark Gable, Gloria Swanson and Jean Harlow. The original hotel was built in 1880 by San Francisco capitalists and the Southern Pacific Railroad. It burned down in April of 1887 and was rebuilt the same year. In October 1924, the center section of the building burned and the "new" Hotel Del Monte opened on May 8, 1926.

2582 – SALMON CATCH. MONTEREY BAY, MONTEREY, CALIFORNIA.

Edw. H. Mitchell, Pub.

Salmon Catch, Monterey Bay, Cal.

M. Reider, Pub.

2727 – Sardine Packing Plant at Monterey, California.

Edw. H. Mitchell, Pub.

"The fishing industry of Monterey has perhaps exceeded the expectations of the early prophets. As one of the principal fishing centers along the Pacific Coast, it supplies sea food for all parts of America and many other parts of the world. The supply of fish in adjacent fishing grounds has seemed inexhaustible. The fishermen may be heard clumping down to their boats in great rubber shoes at all hours of the night. The cannery folk toil through long hours—and at high wages—cutting, sorting, and packing the fish."—R. G. Watkins, *History of Monterey & Santa Cruz Counties, California,* 1925

This two-story adobe was originally owned by Don Rafael Gonzales. It was later known as the French Hotel and owned by Jules Simoneau. Robert Louis Stevenson lived here for several months when he visited Monterey in 1879 and the structure was later renamed in his honor.

2899 - Stevenson House - Monterey, California

Edw. H. Mitchell, Pub.

Detroit Publishing Co.

6457 ROBERT LOUIS STEVENSON HOUSE, MONTEREY, CALIF.

ROBERT LOUIS STEVENSON HOUSE, MONTEREY, CALIFORNIA—M5

Bell Magazine Agency, Pub.

Left: A later view of the Robert Louis Stevenson house, the only remaining house in the West that was occupied by him.

613 — FIRST BRICK HOUSE IN CALIFORNIA AND OLD WHALING STATION.

Edw. H. Mitchell, Pub.

The Whaling Station was erected in 1855 as a boarding house for Portuguese whalers. Whaling lasted in the Monterey Bay for about thirty-five years and then, becoming unprofitable, faded out. The building was later converted into a modern house. The balcony was added in 1903.

This first brick house built in California was erected in 1848 on what is now Decatur Street.

Located at the corner of Pacific and Scott Streets, this "First Theatre" was built by Jack Swan in 1847 and used as a sailor's boarding house. It was converted into a theatre a year later, in 1848.

614 — FIRST THEATRE BUILDING IN CALIFORNIA, MONTEREY.

6460 COLTON HALL, FIRST STATE CAPITOL OF CALIFORNIA, MONTEREY.

Built in 1849 by the Rev. Walter Colton, this two-story adobe was designed as a school and town hall but was to become the first capital of California. Mr. Colton had been appointed *alcalde* on July 28, 1846. He established California's first newspaper, in 1846—the *Californian*.

617 — COLTON HALL—FIRST CAPITOL OF CALIFORNIA, MONTEREY

COLTON HALL 1849 California's "Constitution Hall"

It was here that the people of California set the machinery into motion for a state government under the flag of the United States. This old New England structure was paid for by the fines of gamblers and drunks, and built mostly by slave labor. It now houses the police dep't of

MONTEREY California

W1167

Frashers, Inc., Pub.

Edw. H. Mitchell, Pub.

1148 – Officers' Club, Presidio of Monterey, California.

The Presidio of Monterey was dedicated on June 3, 1770 at the same time as the Mission. A new presidio was established in 1900 by the United States Government as a military post.

3166 – Guard House, Presidio of Monterey, California.

Edw. H. Mitchell, Pub.

Views show soldiers in formation in their fatigue uniforms, at the left, and below, prepared for a drill parade.

1149 – Review at the Presidio of Monterey, California.

Edw. H. Mitchell, Pub.

In 1847 the lumber for this house was brought from Australia to Monterey by William Buston, a sea captain. The house was torn down in 1923...or fell down?

Monterey can boast of many "firsts" and this house was the first in town to have a weather vane atop its roof. Thomas Larkin built this adobe and it was the first state Hall of Records.

1136 – Public Library, Monterey, California.

Edw. H. Mitchell, Pub.

This library, completed in 1911, was designed by William H. Weeks of Watsonville. A new library was constructed in 1952 and the old one is now the Monterey Institute of Foreign Studies.

This first hotel in California, the Washington, stood on the northeast corner of Washington and Pearl Streets. Erected in 1832, it was called the "Del Monte" of old Monterey. At one time the scene of many grand balls, it fell into disrepute and was torn down in 1914.

LITHO. BRITTON & REY, SAN FRANCISCO, CAL. 4304

Britton & Rey, Pub.

OLD WASHINGTON HOTEL, MONTEREY, FIRST HOTEL IN CALIFORNIA

160 — Old Custom House, Monterey, California.

Edw. H. Mitchell, Pub.

This Custom House has flown the flags of three nationalities—Spanish, Mexican, and American. It was built in 1814 and various sections were added later.

B. W. White, Pub.

63 Old Custom House, Monterey, California

"On July 7th, 1846, American flag raised by Commodore John Drake Sloat, signalizing the passing of California from Mexican rule."—on back of post card

28

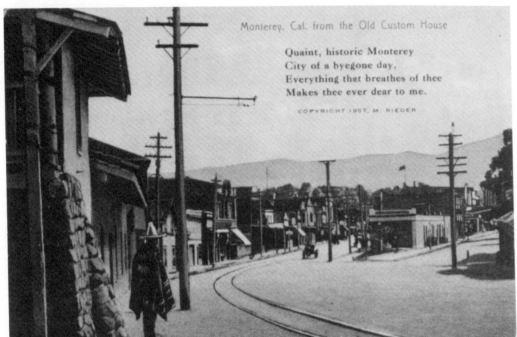

Monterey, Cal. from the Old Custom House

Quaint, historic Monterey
City of a byegone day,
Everything that breathes of thee
Makes thee ever dear to me.

COPYRIGHT 1907, M. RIEDER

M. Reider, Pub.

When California became a state in 1850, Monterey was one of the original counties and the first capital of the new state. Incorporated in 1889, the city progressed and boasted its first telephone and electric lights in 1891.

The street scene on the right pictures the First National Bank. The building was designed by William H. Weeks in 1904. "The new structure will be one of the handsomest interior bank buildings in California. Mr. Weeks has designed a large number of business blocks and residences in the old state capital this year and the work stands as a monument to his skills as an architect."— Evening *Pajaronian*, February 25, 1904

3050 Alvarado Street, Monterey, California.

REAL ESTATE

Edw. H. Mitchell, Pub.

Edw. H. Mitchell, Pub.

Monterey—one of the "leading watering places and resorts of the State." With its rich, historical background, beautiful bay and Spanish town atmosphere, it beckons the visitor from the hot summer inland valleys.

Edw. H. Mitchell, Pub.

30

9670.   A BUSINESS STREET IN MONTEREY, CALIF.

Both of these post cards were published by the Detroit Publishing Company in 1906 and are dated March 29, 1907. On the right, the men are repairing their fishing nets as they prepare to take their boats out onto the bay hoping for a good day's haul.

9558.   THE OLD CUSTOM HOUSE PORCH, MONTEREY, CALIF.

"A hotel I recommend to all my friends."

"Monterey literally bristles with historical interest. Monterey was discovered by Cabrillo, 50 years after Columbus discovered America. Most of the early day charm of California's first capital under the Spanish and later under the Mexican flag is retained in the historical old buildings and homes, relics of a romantic past."—on back of post card

MAIN LOBBY—HOTEL SAN CARLOS, MONTEREY, CALIFORNIA.

115421

Curt Teich & Co., Pub.

Curt Teich & Co., Pub.

Greetings from MONTEREY CALIFORNIA

© CURT TEICH & CO., INC.   ZB-H955

M – Old Customs House
O – Larkin House
N – Colton Hall
T – Ghost Tree, 17 Mile Drive
E – Air View
R – First Theatre in California
E – Hotel San Carlos
Y – Old Mission

568 — MAIN STREET, SALINAS, CALIFORNIA.

Edw. H. Mitchell, Pub.

SALINAS

Salinas, home of the California Rodeo each July, was founded in 1856. Also known as the "Salad Bowl of the World" and "Steinbeck Country," Salinas became the county seat of Monterey County in 1873.

Above: Salinas in horse and buggy days and the dirt streets that were so mucky in the winter. The I.O.O.F. building, erected in 1887, is on the right and just beyond it is the McDougall building where William H. Weeks, architect, had his branch office. Right: A bird's-eye view of Salinas looking toward the Gabilan mountain range.

SALINAS, CAL.   COAST LINE.

Publisher unknown

The second Salinas High School, built in 1900. Damaged by the 1906 earthquake, it was repaired and later became the Central Grammar School. The building was razed in 1937.

High School, Salinas, Cal.

Pacific Novelty Co., Pub.

Wayne Paper Box & Printing Corp., Pub.

The present day high school was built in 1920 and designed by Ralph Wyckoff, who had trained in the office of William H. Weeks.

UNION HIGH SCHOOL, SALINAS, CALIF.   H-780

Salinas Public Library, Salinas, Cal.

The Salinas Public Library was built in 1909 by a grant from Andrew Carnegie of $10,000. Erected on the corner of Main and San Luis Streets, the building became the second unit of the Civic Center in 1960 when the Steinbeck Library was completed. Mrs. Carrie Striening was the librarian in 1909 at a salary of fifteen dollars a month.

Library, Salinas, Cal.

The Salinas City Bank building was erected in 1873 and stood to the left of the Abbott House. The interior of the bank was remodeled in 1899 by architect William H. Weeks. A new building was erected on the corner of Main and Gabilan Streets, shown below.

Main and Gabalan Sts. Salinas, Cal.

4843

Salinas City Bank, Salinas, Cal.

4848

Publisher unknown

Pacific Novelty Co., Pub.

West Gabilan St., Salinas, Cal.   *Alma Eaton*

Newman Post Card Co., Pub.

Ford & Sanborn's General Merchandise Store was opened on August 25, 1868. The bank is on the opposite corner.

The McDougall building, on the right, was designed by William H. Weeks for James McDougall—merchant, postmaster, cattleman and former president of the Salinas City Bank. Built in 1898, the structure still stands at 171 Main Street. Shown on the bottom floor is the Wahrlich Cornett Co. which stocked groceries, provisions, hardware and agricultural implements. C. H. W. Wahrlich headed the firm. This post card is dated 1906.

Publisher unknown

MAIN STREET, N. OF GABILAN ST. SALINAS, CAL.

"When the plans for the Bardin Hospital at Salinas were presented to the generous donor, the main entrance bore the inscription 'James Bardin Hospital.' He said he had been old 'Jim' Bardin for forty years, and it was going to be the 'Jim' Bardin Hospital, and thus the inscription is going to read." (The *Pajaronian*, March 15, 1906) Designed by William H. Weeks, the building was erected at a cost of $52,000 and stood on the corner of Main and John Streets.

Jim Bardin Hospital, Salinas, Cal.

Edw. H. Mitchell, Pub.

JIM BARDIN HOSPITAL, SALINAS, CAL.

Publisher unknown

T. & D. Theatre, and Elk Bldg., Salinas, Cal. 4846

Marquee on the theatre reads, "Now playing—four acts vaudeville—Weds. & Thurs. Katherine MacDonald in *Stranger Then Fiction*."—1921

Publisher unknown

"Well! Here I am: Hotel Jeffery, Salinas, California—the detour point for Santa Cruz Beach, Giant Redwood Trees, historic Monterey, Pacific Grove, Carmel, Point Lobos, Highland Inn and the world renowned Del Monte.

"Hotel Jeffery Ranch Horses appear regularly at the Annual California Rodeo at Salinas—the home of the recognized stockman's show."—on back of card

Publisher unknown

Ranch Horses of Hotel Jeffery, Salinas, California, participating in "Old Spanish Days" at Santa Barbara.

Publisher unknown

Jeffery House, later Jeffery Hotel, was built in 1889. There were sixty rooms, a pleasant office, an elegant bar, a dining room, a private parlor cafe, a ladies' parlor, and wide hallways. In 1899 the rates were $1.25 to $2.00 per day. The site is now the location of the Monterey Savings & Loan Association.

Early day parade showing the Jeffery Hotel in the background and Mrs. Quilty's Boarding House to the right—a two-story building.—Courtesy Mrs. Annie Black

Ford & Sanborn's General Merchandise Store was demolished by the 1906 earthquake and was rebuilt the same year.

Street scene looking north—the T & D, or Fox Theatre is on the far right.

MAIN BUSINESS SECTION. SALINAS. CALIFORNIA.

Albertype Co., Pub.

Publisher unknown

Built in 1900, this house at 418 Pajaro Street was designed by William H. Weeks for Samuel M. Black. Mr. Black had seen a house he liked in Watsonville and asked Weeks to design one similar to it. The house is still standing and is the home of Mrs. Annie Black, widow of Samuel M. Black, Jr.

Mason's Bazaar, Pub.

COURT HOUSE, SALINAS, CAL.

Built in 1878, the Monterey County Court House was designed by L. Goodrich and cost $80,000 to erect. In 1904 architect William H. Weeks was hired to draw up plans for remodeling. This handsome building gave way to more modern and spacious county offices in 1937. Date on post card is 1907.

Some Statistics

Telegraph Line - 1871
Southern Pacific Railroad - 1872
Gas - 1873
Waterworks - 1874
Electricity - 1888
Telephone - 1890
Salinas City Bank founded in 1873
Monterey County Bank in 1890
Salinas Mutual Building & Loan in 1897

Publisher unknown

Salinas, Cal.
5/22/06
Dear Cousin:-
I received your letter today and will answer as soon as I get time. Troop C. was dismissed and we are at home again. Every body is well here.
Arthur & wife & baby are here for a few days.

These post cards are dated 1934 and read, "Cominos Hotel & Grill—On coast highway halfway between San Francisco and San Luis Obispo."

Hotel Cominos—formerly the Abbott House which was built in 1873 by Carlisle S. Abbott. The name can barely be seen at top of the building, below the flag. The Abbott House was designed by James Waters of Watsonville and cost $20,000 to erect—no small sum in those days.

LETTUCE, CARROTS, CELERY, ARTICHOKES, BROCCOLI, TOMATOES

Bell Magazine Agency, Pub.

30,000 CARS OF VEGETABLES SHIPPED ANNUALLY FROM SALINAS, CALIFORNIA   K-334

"This town [Salinas] has a population close on 5,000, it has electric and gas lighting systems, sewers, wide, well cared for paved streets, beautiful residences and church edifices, substantial business blocks, an armory building, city hall, court house, high school, grammar schools, three solid banking houses, and a large number of fine stores thoroughly metropolitan in stocks, displays and fixtures."
—*Central California Illustrated.* (Los Angeles: California Publishing Co., 1899)

The back of this card reads: "Over sixty per cent of the lettuce eaten in the nation comes from the Salinas Valley where they call it 'green gold.' With the longest growing season in the world, heavy shipments are made from April to December and lesser shipments during the other months."

LETTUCE FIELD, SALINAS, CALIFORNIA—51
"SALAD BOWL OF THE NATION"

Wayne Paper Box & Printing Corp., Pub.

HOLLISTER

Named after Colonel William Welles Hollister who, in 1868, sold 21,000 acres of his land to the San Justo Homestead Association—thus the beginning of the town.

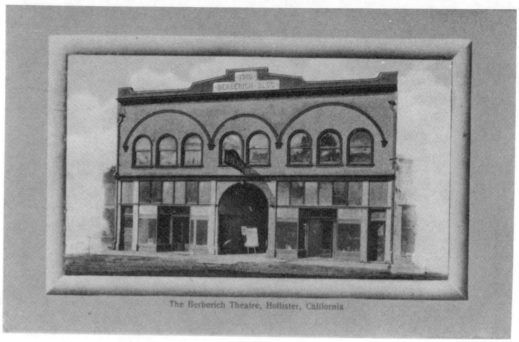

The Berberich Theatre, Hollister, California

Cardinell-Vincent Co., Pub.

Richard Behrendt, Pub.

New Masonic Temple, Hollister, Cal.

The Berberich Theatre, shown above, was built in 1910. The Masonic Temple was erected in 1907-8, designed by William H. Weeks, whose competitive design was chosen over six other architects from San Jose and San Francisco. The dedication was held on October 1, 1908.

1758- High School, Hollister, California

Edw. H. Mitchell, Pub.

"Architect William H. Weeks is rushing to complete the plans for the new San Benito County High School, the prospective of which elicited much favorable comment from the pedagogues of San Francisco last week during the State Teachers' convention."—Evening *Pajaronian*, January 9, 1908. Finished in 1909, the high school's cost of construction was $45,000.

San Juan
Bautista

Mission San Juan Bautista; Founded 1797. 269

Edw. H. Mitchell, Pub.

Pictured here are scenes of the San Juan Fiesta on November 1, 1908, held to raise funds for the Mission.

Publisher unknown

Edw. H. Mitchell, Pub.

Publisher unknown

Central Nave of Mission San Juan Bautista, California.
200 Feet Long, 75 feet wide, 45 feet high

2702A

SPRECKELS, CALIFORNIA.   Spreckels Hotel

SPRECKELS

Claus Spreckels, founder of the Spreckels Sugar Company, opened up a factory in Watsonville in 1888. By 1898 a factory was built in the new town of Spreckels, south of Salinas in Monterey County. The school shown was built in 1899 and designed by William H. Weeks. It was demolished in 1936. The hotel, containing sixty rooms, was erected in 1897.

47. Spreckels School, Salinas, Cal.

Office Building, Spreckels Sugar Co., Spreckels, California

Built in 1897, this office building was designed by William H. Weeks and cost $25,000 to erect.

Wonderful Hot Soda Baths,   Paraiso Hot Springs, Cal.

PARAISO SPRINGS

Hailed as the "Carlsbad of America" was Paraiso Springs. Manager H. C. Shannon was announcing in 1905: "Hot soda and sulphur plunge and tub baths with first class masseurs in attendance. Charming climate, grand scenery and flowers in profusion. Stage meets afternoon train at Soledad and carries you over famous Salinas Valley good roads, a distance of only eight miles." Located on the eastern slope of the Santa Lucia Mountains, the Springs have been a favorite vacation retreat for many years. Architect Weeks designed an addition to the hotel in 1908. The center post card reads: "The fog is in Salinas Valley now and it is grand here. Like it fine - nice guests." Dated August 1, 1922.

Mineral Swimming Pool over ninety feet long, Paraiso Springs, Cal.

Annex and portion of Hotel Grounds, Paraiso Hot Springs, Cal.

Britton & Rey, Pub.

Britton & Rey, Pub.

Britton & Rey, Pub.

Meddaugh, Pub.

KING CITY

King City, founded in 1887 when the Southern Pacific Railroad was extended from Soledad, is located forty-six miles south of Salinas on the east bank of the Salinas River.

Left, the old Railroad Exchange Hotel.

School House at Kings City, Cal.

Newman Post Card Co., Pub.

Right: The message on the card reads: "Arrived at King City 4:15 and was undecided whether to go a little further. But as it was very warm in some towns, decided to engage a room at this hotel and rest and start early in the morning."—c. 1912

Hotel Vendome, King City, Cal.   4897

Pacific Novelty Co., Pub.

Publisher unknown

CITY HALL
GILROY CALIFORNIA 878.

GILROY

Gilroy—named after John Gilroy who settled in the area in 1814 and died in 1869. The town was incorporated in 1868—the same year that Southern Pacific started laying track from San Jose to Gilroy.

The Gilroy City Hall was erected in 1905, designed by architects Wolfe & McKenzie of San Jose. George Dunlop was mayor of Gilroy at the time.

Gilroy, Cal. - Carnegie Public Library.

In August of 1909, plans submitted by architect William H. Weeks were accepted by the town trustees for a new Carnegie Library. Constructed by contractor H. J. Woods of Watsonville on land formerly used as a tennis court, the building cost $10,000. Completed in 1910, it now houses the Gilroy City Museum.

CROWD AT GILROY HOT SPRINGS GREETS THE HUNTER

Pacific Novelty Co., Pub.

Gilroy Hot Springs, Cal.
Some of the Bath Houses.

Pacific Novelty Co., Pub.

The Club House, Gilroy Hot Springs, Cal.

Gilroy Hot Sulphur Springs located twelve miles from town is still a popular place to visit. The post card on the left is dated 1912, which doesn't necessarily mean when it was published, just when it was mailed.

PUBLIC SCHOOL, CASTROVILLE, CAL.

Polychrome Co., Pub.

CASTROVILLE

Founded by Juan B. Castro in 1864, Castroville is laid out on the Castro Grant known as the Bolsa Nueva y Moro Cojo Rancho. Juan was a first cousin of General Jose Castro, one-time governor of California.

The schoolhouse was built in 1895 at a cost of $16,000. Seventeen plans were submitted and the school trustees chose contractor Wilson of Salinas.

Some of the businesses that lined the main street in 1906 were: Walter Wallace's meat market; William James's barber shop; G. A. Martin's blacksmith shop; B. R. Bettencourt's general merchandise store; J. King's barber shop and J. B. Castro, Jr.'s, livery stable.

Known as the "Artichoke Capitol of the World," Castroville has thus become well-known throughout the world.

Edw. H. Mitchell, Pub.

4639 - Street Scene, Castroville, Cal.

TASSAJARA

The hotel was built in 1904 when the springs were under the management of James and Wm. Jeffery of Salinas. The stage would depart from the Jeffery Hotel carrying summer visitors to the springs. In 1949 the resort was gutted by fire then rebuilt. In 1966 it was sold to the Zen Center of San Francisco who still open Tassajara to visitors during the summer months.

M. Reider, Pub.

Santa Lucia Hotel, at Tassajara Hot Springs, Monterey County, Cal.

Albertype Co., Pub.

Publisher unknown

PAINTING BY HARRISON FISHER
ON SANDSTONE ROCK
TASSAJARA HOT SPRINGS
MONTEREY CO., CALIF.

WATSONVILLE

Watsonville—founded in 1852 on a portion of the Bolsa del Pajaro land grant and named after Judge John H. Watson.

Meddaugh, Pub.

Watsonville Depot located on Beach Road at Walker Street. The Railroad Exchange Hotel is on the right.

Lake Watsonville—formed after the turn of the century by damming up the Pajaro River in the summertime. Scene of boat races, picnics, Fourth of July celebrations, band concerts on the floating bandstand, and swimming races. Post card is dated 1907.

Publisher unknown

The Meddaugh photography studio is shown on the right with the family in its 1908 Overland in front of the store at 18 Peck Street. To the left is the Marinovich Building, formerly the Green Block, built in 1899.

Meddaugh, Pub.

Publisher unknown

Post card showing the interior of the Buckhart Candy Store located at 329 Main Street. The two men pictured are Richard and Harry Buckhart. They purchased the McCallum candy store in January of 1904. Buckhart's is now located in Santa Cruz.

Main Street, Watsonville, Cal.

Main Street looking south in 1912. Mansion House on the left was designed by Thomas Beck, former state senator and secretary of state, and was built in 1871. The Charles Ford Company, on the right, was founded in 1852 and is now the oldest operating mercantile store in California.

Main Street in 1906, looking north. Charles Ford Company is on the left and the Mansion House is on the right. This hotel was moved north on Main Street in 1914 to make room for the Lettunich Building built the same year.

MAIN STREET, LOOKING NORTH, WATSONVILLE, CAL.

Cardinell-Vincent Co., Pub.

Steinhauser & Eaton, Pub.

Down through the years Watsonville has been noted for its Fourth of July parades and people have come from neighboring towns to view the colorful floats, the marching units and the bands with their spirited music. The post card shows a portion of the parade in 1907.

Publisher unknown

A replica of Independence Hall in the 1914 parade.

Native Sons and Daughters of the Golden West lined up for the Fourth of July parade in 1909.

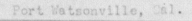

Publisher unknown

Publisher unknown

Publisher unknown

W. THIRD STREET. WATSONVILLE, CAL.

Hailed as one of the "most important seaports on the Pacific Coast," Port Rogers, later called Port Watsonville, was instigated by two promotors from San Jose—W. J. Rogers and H. H. Main. The Watsonville Transportation Company was formed in 1903 and work was begun on the Port—a pier, an electric line from town to the beach, dance hall, cottages, race track, baseball diamond, and a steamer named *Kilburn* (shown above). But the pier kept washing out, the company fell into financial troubles, the property was sold and the whole project finally came to a screeching halt in 1913. Shown on the upper left is the pier and dance pavilion, designed by William H. Weeks. Now the site of Sunset Beach State Park, little remains but a few pilings from the old pier. In the post card on the lower left the streetcar is making its way to the port along West Third, now Beach, Street.

Steinhauser & Eaton, Pub.

One of the "big" ones—the flood of 1911 on the morning of March 7. To the left is the 300 block of Main Street and below right is the city plaza with the Marinovich building in the background and the Pajaro Valley Bank on the right. The post card on the lower left shows a flood scene of Chinatown, which was located in Monterey County just over the Pajaro bridge.

Publisher unknown

Publisher unknown

Steinhauser & Eaton, Pub.

PLAZA, WATSONVILLE, CAL.

Watsonville's city plaza bounded by Main, East Beach, Union and Peck Streets, given to the people of Watsonville by Sebastian Rodriquez in 1860. In the background is the I.O.O.F. building erected in 1893 and designed by T. Lenzen of San Jose. The Opera House, also called Liberty Hall and the Rink, was built in 1871 and designed by James Waters, who was to become one of Watsonville's leading nurserymen. Next is the Linscott house built in 1896, designed by William H. Weeks. It was torn down to make way for a drugstore.

Pacific Novelty Co., Pub.

The Plaza looking North, Watsonville, Cal.   1910

These two pages show more examples of the work of architect William H. Weeks (1864–1936). Weeks had offices in Watsonville, Salinas, San Francisco and Oakland. Although he designed many homes, churches, hotels, office buildings, etc., in Northern California, he was best known for his school designs.

Christian Church—1902. Burned in 1927.

St. Patrick's Catholic Church—1903

Hotel Resetar—1927

Richard Behrendt, Pub.

3rd Street, Watsonville, Cal.

Publisher unknown

Above: William O'Brien home—1905. Warren Porter home—1900. Below: Second high school—1902 (torn down in 1964). Weeks also designed the first high school in 1895 and the present high school in 1917.

Edw. H. Mitchell, Pub.

820 EDWARD H. MITCHELL, PUBLISHER SAN FRANCISCO

HIGH SCHOOL, WATSONVILLE, CALIFORNIA

FORMER HOME OF JUDGE LEE
WATSONVILLE, CA.

Julius Lee Home—1894

This house was built for Richard Pearson in 1901, another one of Weeks' designs. Located at 261 E. Beach Street, it is now the William Volck Memorial Museum, named after the chemist who helped discover the ortho spray to combat the coddling moth attacking the apple trees. The house was left to the Pajaro Valley Historical Association in 1964 by Volck's widow.

Publisher unknown

Steinhauser & Eaton, Pub.

Watsonville's first hospital was founded by Dr. P. K. Watters in 1897. The Watters house, on the right, was built in 1899 and designed by Weeks. It was torn down many years ago. A facade was added to the front of the hospital and the building is used for apartments and Dr. Henrique Nestler's medical offices.

B CENTRE, WATSONVILLE, CALIFORNIA   UNION ST.

To the left, Union Street, looking north towards the Opera House. Notice the hitching rails along the sidewalks. The Opera House, which had gone through various uses, burned down in 1963 while being used as a bowling alley.

Founded in 1899, the Watsonville Woman's Club built their clubhouse in 1917 at 12 Brennan Street. The architect was Ralph Wyckoff and the cost of the building was $6,858.97.

Another building designed by William H. Weeks was the Hotel Appleton in 1911. The structure still stands at the corner of Rodriguez and West Beach but is now called Wall Street Inn. Pictured below is the Appleton Theatre, between the hotel and Ford's, built in 1915 and also designed by Weeks. It became the T & D Theatre and then the State. It is now used as a warehouse by Ford's Department Store.

Hotel Appleton
Watsonville, Cal.
1782

Edw. H. Mitchell, Pub.

Edw. H. Mitchell, Pub.

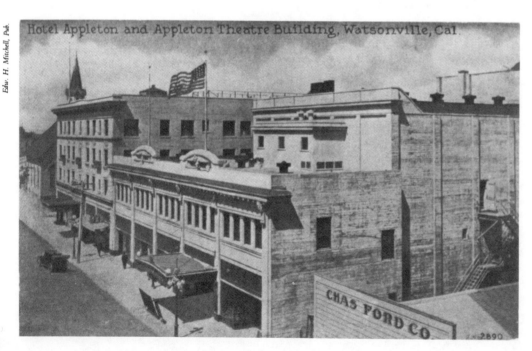

Hotel Appleton and Appleton Theatre Building, Watsonville, Cal.

CHAS FORD CO.

A Corner of The Dining Room of the New Hotel Appleton - Watsonville, California

The dining room, which was located in the corner section, has been converted into a clothing store.

View of the Lobby from Dining Room New Hotel Appleton - Watsonville, California

Publisher unknown

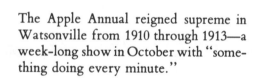

The Apple Annual reigned supreme in Watsonville from 1910 through 1913—a week-long show in October with "something doing every minute."

Post cards on the right and above picture Miss Ruby Brite, Queen of the Apple Show in 1913. She is riding in the patriotic float followed by the city dignitaries in the "white" automobile. Scene is in front of the Pajaro Valley Bank and the City Plaza, with the Mansion House behind.

OUR
APPLE ANNUAL
THE WORLDS GREATEST APPLE SHOW
WATSONVILLE — CALIFORNIA
OCTOBER
10TH TO 15TH

Steinhauser & Eaton, Pub.

Publisher unknown

Steinhauser & Eaton, Pub.

At left is the Apple Annual building designed by William Weeks and finished just in time for the opening of the first show in October 1910. Below left: One of the colorful exhibits displayed inside the auditorium. Shown is a replica of the Casino at Santa Cruz, also designed by Weeks, made of dried and fresh "Santa Cruz Mountain apples."

Edw. H. Mitchell, Pub.

WE CAN CROW ABOUT THE APPLE SHOW WHERE APPLES GROW

AND THE STATE POULTRY SHOW WATSONVILLE CALIFORNIA OCTOBER 9TH TO 14TH

Publisher unknown

Santa Cruz Mountain Apples

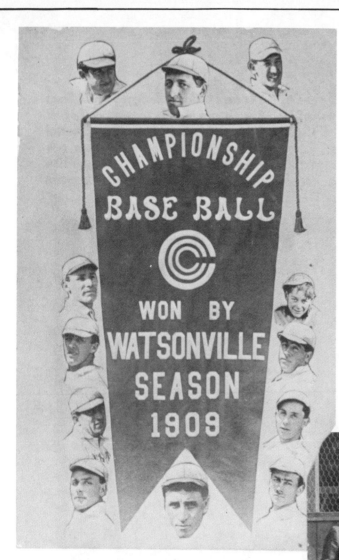

Steinhauser & Eaton, Pub.

"Pippins white washed Monterey Barracudas yesterday in one of the season's greatest games."—Evening *Pajaronian,* October 11, 1909

Publisher unknown

Watsonville had won the Three "C" League Pennant at the end of a "tough, hard-fought, brilliant, spectacular" six-months season, in front of 2,500 spectators on October 10. Other towns in the league were Monterey, Salinas, Hollister, Santa Cruz and San Jose. Top hitter for the season was pitcher Friene with a .340 average; close behind was first baseman Sears with .321 and catcher Grant with .315. Local diamond was located on the corner of Walker and Ford Streets. From left: Tom Albright, manager, Ray Bartlett, Frank Sears, Lynn Marsh, Charles Friene, Joe Giannini, Chris Gorman, Vic Salsberg, Mr. Sherman, Pancho Dias, Joe Nevis and Sid Smith.

From left: Tom Albright, manager, Ray Bartlett, Frank Sears, Lynn Marsh, Charles Friene, Joe Giannini, Chris Gorman, Vic Salsberg, Mr. Sherman, Pancho Dias, Joe Nevis and Sid Smith.

Post cards on this page courtesy of the Pajaro Valley Historical Association.

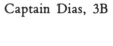

Captain Dias, 3B

Publisher unknown

THIS IS THE KIND WE GROW in Salinas

These fanciful post cards reflected the pride of farmers in Salinas, "the nation's salad bowl," and Watsonville, famous for its October Apple Annual.

2189 — A CARLOAD OF MAMMOTH STRAWBERRIES FROM

2184 — A CARLOAD OF RED APPLES FROM

S.P. 79482

Copyright 1910 by Edward H. Mitchell, San Francisco.

Edw. H. Mitchell, Pub.

S.P. 79295

Copyright 1910 by Edward H. Mitchell, San Francisco.

Edw. H. Mitchell, Pub.

On October 11, 1912, the government submarine F-1 broke its cable while anchored off Port Watsonville for the Apple Annual festivities. Two men were washed off the deck by pounding breakers and drowned. Fourteen other crewmen were rescued as the submarine tossed and thrashed while locked on the sand bar that early foggy morning.

"The submarine F-1 was pulled off the sands by the battleship *Maryland* and the tugs *Iroquois* and *Vigilante*. This afternoon the tugs will leave for Vallejo with the submarine, which will have to be completely overhauled and repaired at the Mare Island Navy Yard."—*Evening Pajaronian*, October 19, 1912

Edw. H. Mitchell, Pub.

2474 – SOUTHERN PACIFIC DEPOT, CAPITOLA, CALIFORNIA.

CAPITOLA

Frederick A. Hihn laid out Capitola in 1868 and the first train came to town in 1876. Depot shown is now being used as a private home.

Charles Weidner, Pub.

Street Scene in Capitola Santa Cruz County California.

509

Capitola By the Sea, California.   6228

Pacific Novelty Co., Pub.

Edw. H. Mitchell, Pub.

1473 — SOUTHERN PACIFIC FLYER CROSSING THE RIVER NEAR CAPITOLA, CALIFORNIA.

Post card is dated 1911 and reads: "Dear Ma – Am having good time down here. Fine swimming. There is about 1,000 people here. Hattie & Ad."

547 Bathing at Capitola, SANTA CRUZ COUNTY, California.

Charles Weidner, Pub.

188 — BIRDS-EYE VIEW OF CAPITOLA, CALIFORNIA.

Edw. H. Mitchell, Pub.

The Capitola Hotel, containing 160 rooms, was built in 1895 and was considered one of the finest on the coast. It was consumed by fire in 1929.

Main Street. Capitola, Cal.

4061—Beach and Hotel at Capitola, Near Santa Cruz, California.

Publisher unknown

The post card on the left shows San Jose Avenue in Capitola and the writer says, "Here's where I am staying, it's the 'old Schwartz' cottage." Dated 1922.

THE CHUTES, CAPITOLA, CALIFORNIA   5943

Publisher unknown

Publisher unknown

Dated 1936

CHILDREN'S POOL ON THE BEACH CAPITOLA, CALIFORNIA

Publisher unknown

It is Certainly a Long
Time Since You Were in

Soquel

Can't You Come Now

SOQUEL

Soquel had its beginnings as a township in 1852, the same year as its neighbor, Watsonville. The first general store was opened in 1853 by Edward F. Porter, who was also the first postmaster.

Postmarked 1913.

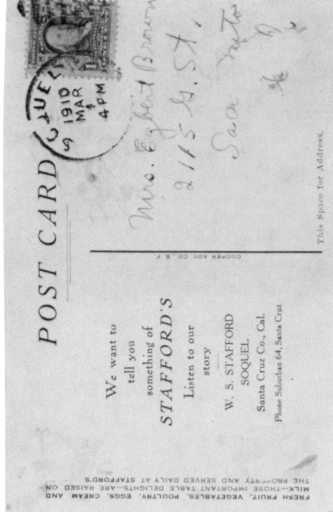

The Stafford Hotel was located in Soquel and had extensive grounds for the raising of fresh foods for its guests.

Bottom post card reads: "Just a note to tell you that we are holding a golf tournament over the Labor Day holidays. We will be glad to see you at any time. Tennis and golf are our special ties. We also have a fine string of saddle horses. Cordially, Prescott's Inn." Dated 1930.

Santa Cruz

HAPPY NEW YEAR!

Fifth Annual Flower Show at Santa Cruz, California

SANTA CRUZ CALIFORNIA

Santa Cruz Dept. of Events, Pub.

"On the beach at Santa Cruz, California, January 1, 1928. Can you imagine it? Here it is New Year's Day and hundreds of people are on the beach enjoying a picnic and men are swimming in the surf? The Fifth Annual New Year's Flower Show is being held in the Auditorium at the beach overlooking beautiful Monterey Bay. There are over 150 different varieties of flowers on display and all have been grown out of doors. Then there is the baby vehicle parade from the Casa del Rey hotel gardens to the Auditorium. Scores of pretty babies in buggies and go-carts decorated with flowers. The gathering on the beach is termed the Picnic of the States and Californians greet people who have come from other states to live in Santa Cruz. Sunshine, flowers, bathing, boating, golfing, fishing and many other kinds of events on New Year's Day in Santa Cruz! What a wonderful place in which to live."—on back of card

BEACH AND BATH HOUSE, SANTA CRUZ, CAL.

M. Rieder, Pub.

In 1893, John Leibrandt and Captain C. F. Miller built a bathhouse with indoor sea water pool. Horsedrawn cars carried passengers between the beach and the town.

Built in 1904, this first Casino was designed by architect E. L. Van Cleeck. The contractor was F. K. Cummings and the price was $33,276. It burned down on June 6, 1906.

NEPTUNE CASINO, SANTA CRUZ, CALIFORNIA

Edw. H. Mitchell, Pub.

The Pleasure Pier was constructed in 1904 at a cost of $1,000 and was torn down in 1962.

Architect William H. Weeks drew the plans for this second Casino for the newly formed Santa Cruz Beach, Cottage and Tent Corporation. The main floor contained the main room and sixteen booths and concessions including a barber shop. A theatre on the second floor could seat from 2,500 to 4,000 people.

3259 - The Casino from the Beach, Santa Cruz, California.

Edw. H. Mitchell, Pub.

The Casino opened in June of 1907 - "The festive summer season at Santa Cruz went into full swing with a great blaze of glory Saturday night, when the monster Casino was formally opened..."—Evening *Pajaronian*, June 17, 1907

"At the new Casino Theatre - An audience befitting the play, a play befitting a brilliant auditorium. Manager Swanton and architect Weeks, the Beach Company, Nance O'Neil and her company, and the people of Santa Cruz may remember Monday night, July 1, 1907, as a proud night. The tiers of boxes were filled with elegant costumes, and the graceful drooping ostrich plumes, so high in fashion's favor this season, were conspicuous in all parts of the house."—Santa Cruz *Surf*, July 2, 1907

Ball Room-Casino, Santa Cruz, Cal.

Newman Post Card Co., Pub.

This post card showing the interior of the Casino is dated October 17, 1909. This is now the Penny Arcade and the interior decor has changed just a little!

Britton & Rey, Pub.

4639—Interior of the Casino. Santa Cruz, C

Detroit Publishing Co.

THE TENT CITY, SANTA CRUZ, CAL.

Tent City – 200 units built in 1903 by Fred Swanton behind the first Casino and Natatorium.

Newman Post Card Co., Pub.

Cottage City and Casino, Santa Cruz, Cal.

In December of 1906, W. H. Weeks was preparing plans for one hundred cottages to be built to the rear of the second Casino. This was later to become the site of the Casa del Rey Hotel. Cottages ranged in size from one to three rooms.

Cottage City, Santa Cruz, Cal. 2084

Pacific Novelty Co., Pub.

Casa del Rey Hotel. Built in 1911 by Fred Swanton, it contained 300 rooms, extensive gardens, and one could walk through the archway to the ballroom at the Casino. The card on the right is dated 1914 and says: "Rates lower this year and the water's fine. Come on." The card below states: "This is a beautiful room, the sun just pours in here all day. The hotel is very pretty."

Casa del Rey, Santa Cruz, Cal.

Souvenir Publishing Co.

Pacific Novelty Co., Pub.

Sun Room, Casa del Rey, Santa Cruz, Cal.   2073

4066—Casa del Rey, Santa Cruz, California.

Cardinell-Vincent Co., Pub.

The Boardwalk at Santa Cruz.

Publisher unknown

Entrance to Casa del Rey Hotel near California's Finest Beach, Santa Cruz. Famous for its Atmosphere of Gracious Hospitality and Service.

The cards at left and below are from an original painting by E. A. Burbank, internationally known artist, 1928. The card at left reads, "Dearest Mildred: So good you have been to us. Everything arrived—corsets, hanky, pictures, books, etc. I'll write you a letter on the boat. Too busy these days having a fine week-end here at Santa Cruz. Doris and Jim." Dated December 29, 1929.

Auditorium at the Beach, Santa Cruz, California, Scene of Many Conventions, Connected With Casa del Rey Hotel by Covered Bridge.

Santa Cruz, Calif.

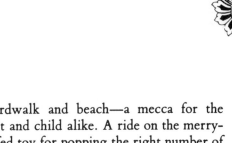

Santa Cruz boardwalk and beach—a mecca for the vacationer—adult and child alike. A ride on the merry-go-round, a stuffed toy for popping the right number of balloons, or some of the famous salt water taffy—it's all still there. The boards are gone and you now walk on a cement "boardwalk," some of the games and rides have been changed over the years, but it's still one of the favorite playlands on the West Coast.

The ship *Balboa* anchored out in the bay in 1907. This pleasure ship featured gambling and prostitution, illegal on shore according to John Chase in his book *The Sidewalk Companion to Santa Cruz Architecture*. Visitors were brought to the *Balboa* from the pleasure pier on the speedboat *Sinaloa* which belonged to Sunday Farola.

4042—The Surf at Santa Cruz, showing the "Balboa" in the distance. Cal.

Britton & Rey, Pub.

3127. Waiting for Life Buoys.

"The lower left of this card shows part of a train tunnel and the ticket booth where a ticket could be purchased for ten cents for a ride on the boardwalk. The popcorn machine next to the booth had the best fresh popcorn around for five cents a bag. The middle of the card shows the C. Stagnaro fishing trip ticket booth. Across the wharf from that was the Ideal Fish Restaurant which at the time was owned by a Mr. Waterman. Goebel's Fish Market next to the Ideal was run by George Goebel, his wife, his sister, and Nick Bassano. The Ideal's Annex was next to the fish market. The annex was just an extension of the restaurant where you could eat and watch the action on Cowell's beach. The pier bathhouse at the right of the picture was owned by a Mrs. Boswick. She was one of the biggest landowners in Santa Cruz at that time. The bushes at the lower right of the card show the present site of the Terrace Court."—information provided by Joan Stagnaro, wife of Robert "Big Boy" Stagnaro

Publisher unknown

Goebel's at the Wharf

Janssen Litho Co., Pub.

The Bayside Lodge was located at 34 First Street and was run by Mrs. F. W. Chapin. The post card is dated 1916 and was written by people who stayed in the furnished rooms while visiting from Sacramento, California.

The Sea Beach Hotel at Santa Cruz, California.

"The Omega Nus, the Girls' Sorority, know how to entertain and their party on New Year's Eve was a great success. It was held at the Sea Beach Hotel and the ball room was a dream."—Santa Cruz *Surf*, January 2, 1904

Originally the site of the Douglas House, which was purchased by D. K. Abeel in 1886 and enlarged into the newly-named Sea Beach Hotel. This hotel was to burn down in a spectacular fire on June 12, 1912 at 3 A.M.— only a small dance hall was saved. It had been conducted by J. J. C. Leonard, who also managed the St. George Hotel, downtown Santa Cruz.

Edw. H. Mitchell, Pub.

319   Burning of the Sea Beach Hotel, Santa Cruz, California.

Pacific Novelty Co., Pub.

Santa Cruz County National Bank, Santa Cruz   1936

This building, which houses the County Bank of Santa Cruz, founded in 1870, was remodeled in 1910 by Weeks. The cupola, along with the corner entrance at Pacific and Front, were removed. The post card is dated 1913.

Mission Hill School was built in 1876 on the former site of the Pope House. The school was remodeled and the third floor and a cupola were removed. The build... was town down in 1930.

The People's Bank at 1515 Pacific Avenue was built in 1910 and designed by William H. Weeks. The building now houses shops and an ice cream parlor and lunch room.

"Santa Cruz Mission was founded in the same year as Mission 'La Soledad'—1791. In January 1840, an earthquake and tidal wave partially destroyed the building. The final disaster occurred in 1851 when the walls fell. The Mission has now entirely disappeared."

The present Mission replica was constructed in 1932 (not shown).

Edw. H. Mitchell, Pub.

Santa Cruz Mission, California, 1791.   Z 19

Edw. H. Mitchell, Pub.

1754 - Holy Cross School, Santa Cruz, California.

Day School, Boarding School, Orphanage—this School of the Holy Cross was founded by the Sisters of Charity in 1862. The first small wooden building, on the left, was built in 1865 and designed by Thomas Beck. The building on the right was designed in 1890 by T. J. Welch. Both buildings were razed in 1944.

Seaside Store, Santa Cruz, California.

2253

This store was incorporated into the present day Leask's Department Store. Samuel Leask, Sr., bought out George Place, owner of the Seaside Store, in 1892. A new building was designed by Weeks and constructed in 1906.

Hotel Furrer—100 Beach Street, Santa Cruz. James & Mary Furrer, managers. Message on back of card reads: "Dear Ma: I am going to stay until Saturday. I have paid up to then already. Your Son, C.L.V." Dated 1914.

HOTEL FURRER

HOTEL FURRER

HOTEL FURRER - AT THE BEACH - SANTA CRUZ CALIFORNIA

Santa Cruz Post Office—built in 1911 at the corner of Water, Pacific, and Front. Former site of the Swanton House which burned in 1887.

Edw. H. Mitchell, Pub.

Post Office, Santa Cruz, California.

2252

Publisher unknown

RIVERSIDE HOTEL
SANTA CRUZ, CALIFORNIA.

The Riverside Hotel was built by Fred Barson in 1870 on thirty acres of land. Remodeled in 1877, the hotel was in its heyday in the early part of the century with its own gardens, orchard and dairy. The cuisine was excellent and the hotel was well-known for its accommodations and its genial hosts.

O. Newman Co., Pub.

RIVERSIDE HOTEL, SANTA CRUZ, CAL.

Another view of the Riverside Hotel. The postcard below, dated August 25, 1909, says: "The weather here is glorious. Much better than Pacific Grove. We are greatly enjoying it."

Lobby of Riverside Hotel, Santa Cruz, California

O. Newman Co., Pub.

This postcard tells quite a bit about early day transportation with its bicycle rider, horse-drawn cart and one of those "new-fangled" automobiles! The Unique Theatre on the right was built in 1904. It became a movie theatre in later years and was torn down in 1936.

Field & Cole Company owned by Robert Field, J. W. Dickinson and Charles A. Cole. Located at 188 Pacific Avenue, there were also branches at the Casino and in Capitola.

Richard Behrendt, Pub.

Court House. Santa Cruz, Cal.

The Santa Cruz County Court House was erected in 1895 and rebuilt under the direction of Thomas Beck after the 1906 earthquake. When the present court house was built the old building was sold to Max Walden, who converted it into shops, a bar, and a restaurant in 1969. (Now called Cooper House)

Court House, Santa Cruz, Cal.

Newman Post Card Co., Pub.

J. Bogdan, Pub.

Charles Weidner, Pub.

516 High School, SANTA CRUZ, California.

Santa Cruz's first high school building was constructed in 1895 and dedicated the same year on July 19. The school burned down in 1913 and was replaced with the present structure.

High School, Santa Cruz, Cal.

79

"W. H. Weeks, the eminent architect, was in town Saturday on business connected with the erection of the new high school and new Branciforte grammar school buildings. Mr. Weeks recently completed a high school building at Orland, Glenn County, and has the Monterey high school almost completed."—Santa Cruz *Morning Sentinel*, October 4, 1914

Hailing it as the "High School of the Future," Governor Hiram Johnson spoke at the first meeting held in the new high school auditorium on October 7, 1915: "In masterly and convincing oratory people respond with attention and applause and meanwhile extend their chests with pride over the new high school."—Santa Cruz *Sentinel*, October 8, 1915

Wave Motor. Santa Cruz, Cal.

Built just before the turn of the century by the Armstrong Brothers, this wave motor provided water for the sprinkling of streets in Santa Cruz. Situated on the West Cliff Drive, it forced water into a tunnel and up into a storage tank, thus making sea water a usable product in the everyday life of the town.

Arrival of Train, Santa Cruz, Cal.

Pacific Novelty Co., Pub.

Surf Bathing in the Pacific.

Santa Cruz, Cal.

Newman Post Card Co., Pub.

106

3128 — A Seaside Convention.

Edw. H. Mitchell, Pub.

INKY DINKS

Santa Cruz is good enough for me.

Never a dull moment.

Inky Dink

Pacific Novelty Co., Pub.

1457 — SHORE LINE LIMITED, SANTA CRUZ, CALIFORNIA.

Edw. H. Mitchell, Pub.

Scenic Railway, Santa Cruz, California

Field & Cole Curio Co., Pub.

Rotograph Co., Pub.

F. L. 420

CHILLY.

Copyright 1907
By The Rotograph Co., N.Y.

T405. TWO STRINGS TO HER BEAUX.   DETROIT PUBLISHING CO.

From Santa Cruz
Mrs. Cohene + D.

Detroit Publishing Co.

Cardinell-Vincent Co., Pub.

CAMP LIFE IN THE SANTA CRUZ MOUNTAINS 4072

Santa Cruz Mountains

BROOKDALE

Publisher unknown

SULLIVAN CASTLE
Ben Lomond, Calif.

HOWDEN CASTLE, BEN LOMOND, CALIFORNIA   6267

"Weatherly Castle—Highway 9—Ben Lomond, Calif.
This famous tourist attraction overlooks the San Lorenzo
River in the beautiful Santa Cruz Mountains. Weatherly
Castle is open to the public."

Publisher unknown

The Last Ox Team in Santa Cruz Co.—1910.   3067-Laws

Pacific Novelty Co., Pub.

FIRST PONY EXPRESS OFFICE BETWEEN MONTEREY AND SAN FRANCISCO AT BIG TREES,

SANTA CRUZ, CALIF.   SC-308

"The Giant Redwoods (Sequoia Sempervirens) are often 350 feet high and are from 60 to 70 feet in circumference. These trees are estimated to be about 4,000 years old and are perhaps the oldest living things on the earth. The redwoods can be seen in Santa Cruz County conveniently and easily by railroad or auto."

Big Tree Club House, Big Tree Grove near Santa Cruz, Cal.

General Fremont, Wife and Daughter, at the Big Tree Grove, on the Coast Line, between Los Angeles and San Francisco, via Santa Cruz.

Meddaugh, Pub.

Felton was laid out in 1868 by Edward Stanley and named after Stanley's lawyer, Charles Felton. The Grand Central Hotel, in the background of the bottom card, was built in the 1880s. The railroad from Santa Cruz to Felton was opened in 1875.

Part of Felton, California 2321

Souvenir Publishing Co.

Zayante Inn and Station at Mt Hermon, Cal. 368

MEMORIAL CHAPEL
— A delightful, rustically simple place for prayer, song, and worship, this chapel was built by the families of three Mount Hermon young people who have been "called home" and was dedicated to their memory May 30, 1948. It has a seating capacity of 100 people.

The Mt. Hermon Association was formed in 1905. The Zayante Inn burned down in 1921. The beautiful grounds have been expanded over the years—a favorite place for church seminars and conferences.

BROOK IN DINING ROOM, BROOKDALE LODGE,
SANTA CRUZ MOUNTAINS, BROOKDALE, CALIF.

Dated 1925, the above post card reads: "Brookdale Lodge—Dr. F. K. Camp, Proprietor. In the heart of the Big Tree country. Come linger with us, and listen to the song of the brook singing merrily through our dining room." Built in 1923 by Dr. Camp, the lodge, after various ownerships, burned down in 1956, although the dining room is still functional.

These pictures were taken by James E. Meddaugh, Watsonville photographer, who also published the post cards.

FIVE DOLLARS FINE FOR RIDING OR DRIVING ···
··· OVER THIS BRIDGE FASTER THAN A WALK

25

Boulder Creek Cal. Meddah Foto

Boulder Creek Cal. Meddah Foto 23

Main St. Boulder Creek Cal. Meddah Foto. 20

Meddaugh, Pub.

The Boulder Creek High School was built in 1905 and designed by architect William H. Weeks.

Meddaugh, Pub.

Boulder Creek
Meddah Foto

MISCELLANEOUS

The steamer *Gipsy*, also known as "Old Perpetual Motion," crashed on the rocks off McAbee Beach, Monterey, on September 27, 1905. The wreckage of the $20,000 ship was sold at auction for $36. Commanded by Captain Thomas Boyd, the Pacific Coast Line steamer lost its way when a light at New Monterey was mistaken for the wharf light at Monterey. The officers and crew got safely ashore but the once proud little ship was a total disaster.

WRECK OF GIPSY PACIFIC GROVE, CAL. SEPT. 28, 05.

Dear Gertrude:
will send you this card now and will write a letter just as soon as I can find time. am very busy now glad you had such a good time at the picnic. Yours Richie.

WRECK OF THE LA FELIZ   SANTA CRUZ   CALIFORNIA

"Conjecture surrounding the cause of the grounding of the *La Feliz* in a night free from fog and in an atmosphere of good visibility may be somewhat dissipated when the exact nature of tide and off-shore swells of the last two days is fully revealed. The crowd grouped on the brink of the 125-foot cliff watching the work of rescuing of the *La Feliz* crew between twelve and one o'clock last night presented a weirdly picturesque scene. There were plenty of honest-to-goodness heroes last night—we have to include among those Sheriff Trafton and Dick Rountree." (Santa Cruz *Evening News*, October 2, 1924) Just a year later, Sheriff Trafton and Dick Rountree would both be killed in a gun battle at Seacliff in Santa Cruz. After spectators had helped themselves to the beached cans of sardines, the crew salvaged the rest of the cargo and equipment and the ship was abandoned on Monterey Bay's north shore.

Diamond Series, Pub.

Message on post card reads: "Dear friend: I send you this card to tell you that you are on table committee for Friday eve. Cora told me to ask you to bring cake. Be sure and come and get everybody out on your road. With best wishes, Flora"

Pacific Novelty Co., Pub.

ENTRANCE, WATSONVILLE, CALIFORNIA   6877

"On Monterey Peninsula, there are three organized communities—Monterey, Pacific Grove and Carmel. In addition to these there is the Hotel del Monte and their properties. Monterey is one of the most picturesque of American Cities. It is known as the city of three flags and the cradle of California's history and romance. Pacific Grove is a beautiful city of homes, on the northern top of the peninsula. Carmel is a picturesque town located in a dense pine forest with a beautiful bay frontage and a mountainous background."—on back of post card

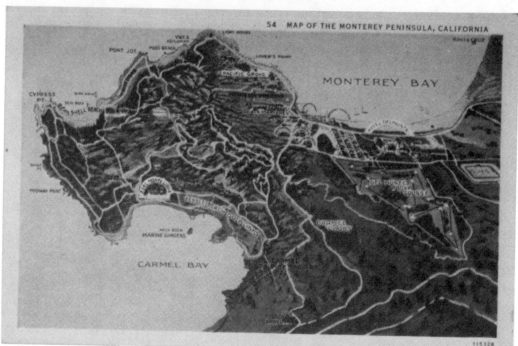

This Chinese fishing village was completely destroyed by fire in 1906.

Hollister

Oct. M. P. Olsen

THE LATHROP BUILDING, A TWO STORY BRICK, AFTER THE QUAKE OF
ABR 18TH 1906. HOLLISTER CAL.

1906 - April 18

SEELY RANCH NEAR AROMAS, CAL.

THE HEAD INN

THE HEAD INN AND GRILL

THE HEAD INN, SOLEDAD.
MONTEREY COUNTY, CALIFORNIA.
NOTED FOR ITS UNEXCELLED CUISINE AND SELECT ACCOMMODATIONS FOR MOTORISTS.
C.S.A.A. OFFICIAL HOTEL—130 MILES FROM SAN FRANCISCO

Typical grade school, Soledad, Monterey County, California

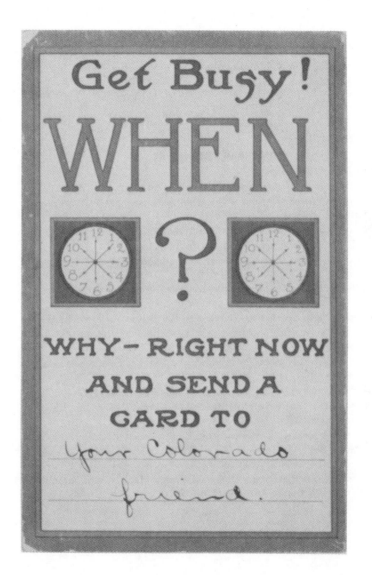

List of Sources

Books and Magazines

Architect & Engineer. 1907–1936.

Central California Illustrated. Los Angeles: California Publishing Co., 1899.

Chase, John. *The Sidewalk Companion to Santa Cruz Architecture.* Santa Cruz: Santa Cruz Historical Society, 1975.

Early Theatres of California. Book Club of California, 1974 Keepsake Series.

Hawkins, T. S. *Some Recollections of a Busy Life.* 1913.

Hicks, John, and Hicks, Regina. *Cannery Row—A Pictorial History.* Creative Books, 1972.

Johnston, Robert B. *Old Monterey County—A Pictorial History.* Monterey: Monterey Savings and Loan Association, 1970.

Koch, Margaret. *Santa Cruz County—Parade of the Past.* Fresno: Valley Publishers, 1973.

Martin, Edward. *History of Santa Cruz, California.* 1911.

Monterey's Adobe Heritage. Monterey: Monterey Savings and Loan Association, 1965.

Pierce, Marjorie. *East of the Gabilans.* Fresno: Valley Publishers, 1977.

Reinstedt, Randall A. *Shipwrecks and Sea Monsters of California's Central Coast.* Ghost Town Publications, 1975.

Sunset. "Monterey County, California." *The Pacific Monthly,* 1912.

Watkins, Major Rolin G. *History of Monterey & Santa Cruz Counties, California.* Chicago: S. J. Clarke Publishing Co., 1925.

The Writers' Group of Canterbury Woods Retirement Home. *Canterbury Chapbooks.* Monterey: d'Angelo Publishing Co., 1968.

Newspapers

Evening Pajaronian
Gilroy Advocate
Hollister Advance
Hollister Free Lance
Monterey Cypress
Monterey Peninsula Herald
Pacific Grove Review
Pacific Grove Tribune
Register Pajaronian
Salinas Californian
Salinas Index
Salinas Journal
Santa Cruz Sentinel
Santa Cruz Surf
Valley World (Gilroy)
Watsonville Register

Institutions, Organizations, and Individuals

California Historical Society Library - San Francisco
Betty Weeks Clark
Barbara Hopkins Davis
Gilroy City Museum
Alice Weeks Halsall
Hollister Library
Monterey County Library
Jack Novcich
Octagon County Museum - Santa Cruz
Pacific Grove Library
Pajaro Valley Historical Association
Esther Steinbeck Rodgers
San Francisco Public Library
Santa Cruz Library
Sam Stark
John Steinbeck Library
Watsonville Public Library
William Volck Memorial Museum